This book is
dedicated to Herb,
Neato and Honey.
The best dogs we've
ever known.

Well Dressed Dogs

A celebration of canine couture

Daniel Aulsebrook & Heather Lighton

Harper *by* Design

About the Authors.

Heather Lighton and Dan Aulsebrook run the boutique dog photography studio Dog Photog (dogphotog.com.au), in Melbourne, Australia. They say: 'We don't just photograph dogs, we pour our total creative selves into finding the inner personality of every dog.'

Heather is a photographer with a background in fine arts, graphic design and styling. She shoots fashion, lifestyle and portraiture, and her photo books are stocked internationally. Heather is also an exhibited artist and has twice participated in the Tokyo Art Book Fair. She is an animal lover and advocate, and is the creative force behind Dog Photog.

Dan has a Bachelor of Arts (Photography) from RMIT in Melbourne, and received a scholarship to study at Parsons in Paris. He enjoys photographing architecture and also dogs. He is the lighting and Photoshop whiz behind Dog Photog. Dan's work has appeared in numerous architecture magazines and design sites.

Heather and Dan live with rescue chihuahua Honey Del Rey – their in-house model and muse – and usually another foster dog or two, and spend every spare minute thinking about ways to photograph dogs. They say: 'Dog Photog has completely taken over our lives – in a good way!'

We really love dogs.

In fact, it's probably more accurate to say we are OBSESSED with all dogs: big dogs, little dogs, curly-haired dogs, three-legged dogs, sleepy dogs, 'I can't stop running in circles' dogs. Honestly, we can't walk down the street without frequently stopping for pats and chats with the dogs (and humans) we encounter.

Way back in 2014 BD (Before Dog Photog), we were both working as 'human photographers', Heather shooting portraiture and fashion while Dan focused on architecture and lifestyle. We wondered (a) why there weren't more photos of dogs that incorporated fun fashion and design elements, and (b) whether it was possible to combine these passions. Luckily, we had two rescue whippets at home – Herb and Neato – to test our ideas on, as well as a revolving door of beautiful foster dogs.

Our new venture, Dog Photog, went live with a pop-up Christmas portrait session. It was a strange assortment of curtains and tinsel but, after years of thinking and talking, it was happening. Over the past nine years our shoots have become more elaborate and Heather now makes all the props and costumes.

In *Well-Dressed Dogs*, we have gathered some of our favourite themes and models to share the joy and cuteness of these sartorial pooches we've been lucky enough to photograph.

Heather & Dan

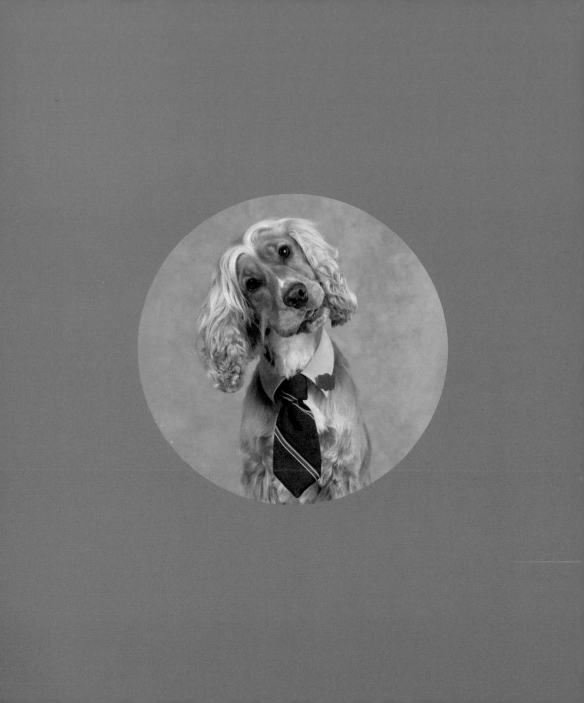

STUDENT COUNCIL

My mum let me get highlights and lowlights.

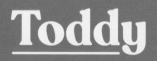

Toddy

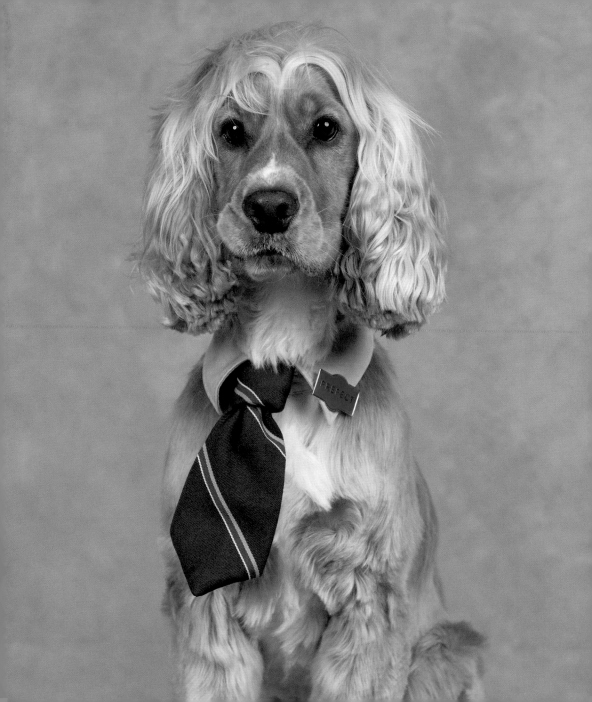

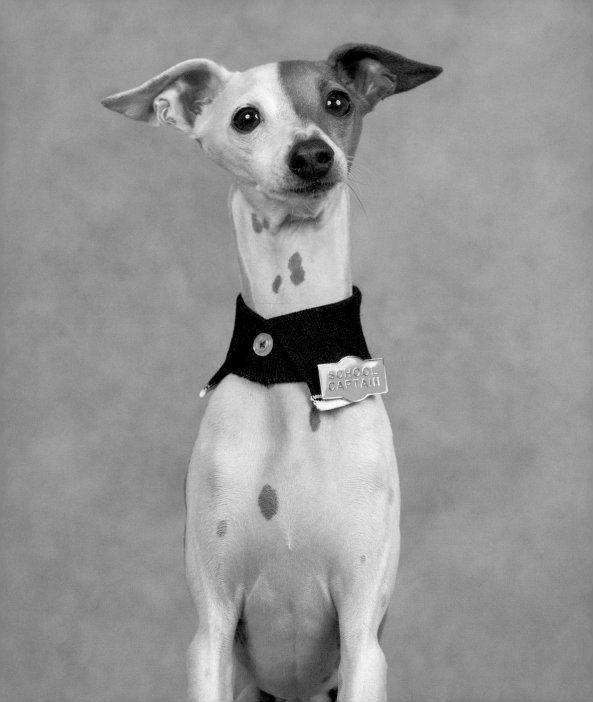

I'd like to be a bad boy ... just once.

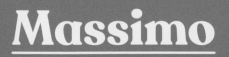

<u>Massimo</u>

I take my student librarian role very seriously.

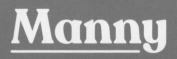

Manny

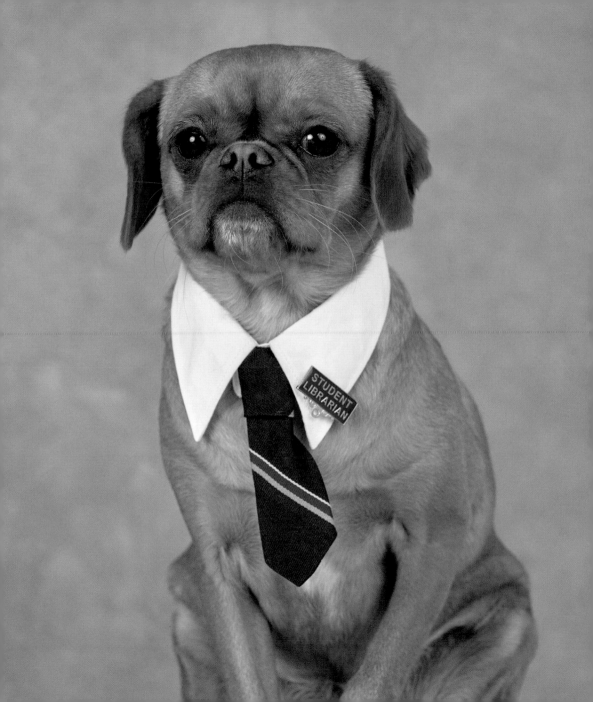

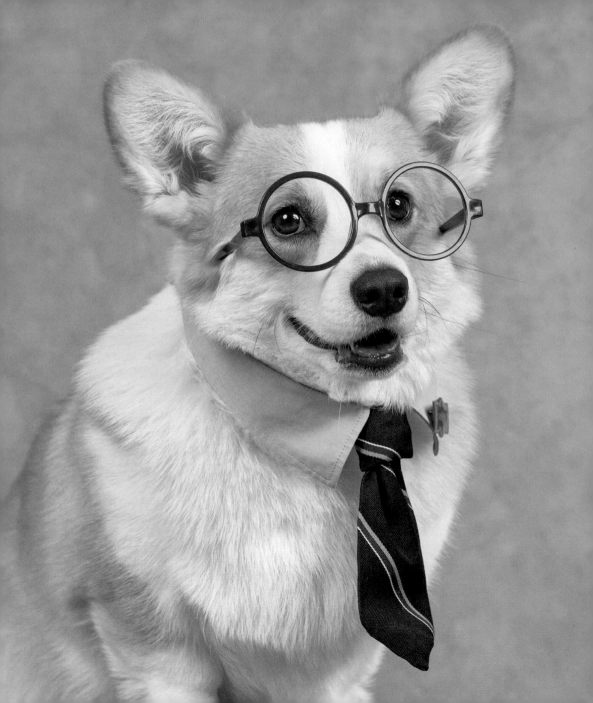

Top of the class ... again.

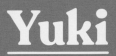

Yuki

School-photo day is totally uncool.

Roy

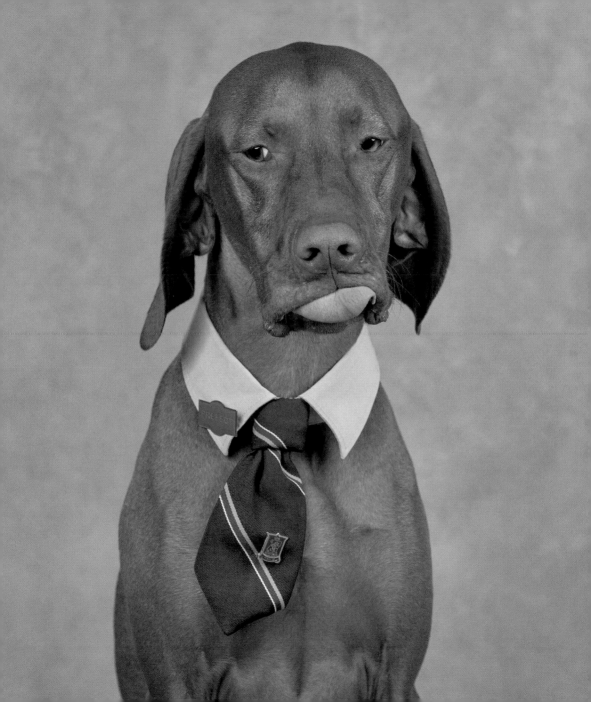

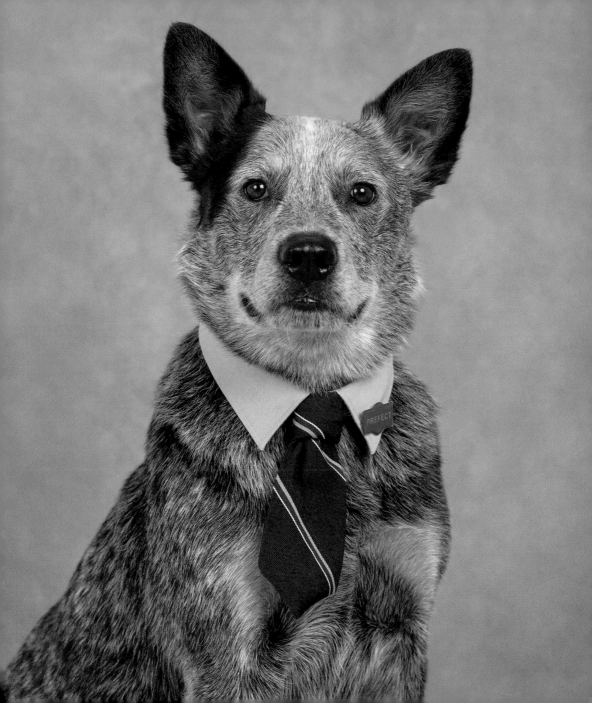

Did I become Head Prefect because I'm incredibly good-looking? Quite possibly.

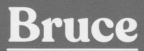

Bruce

Voted 'longest snoot at school' for the fifth year running.

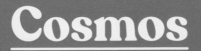

Cosmos

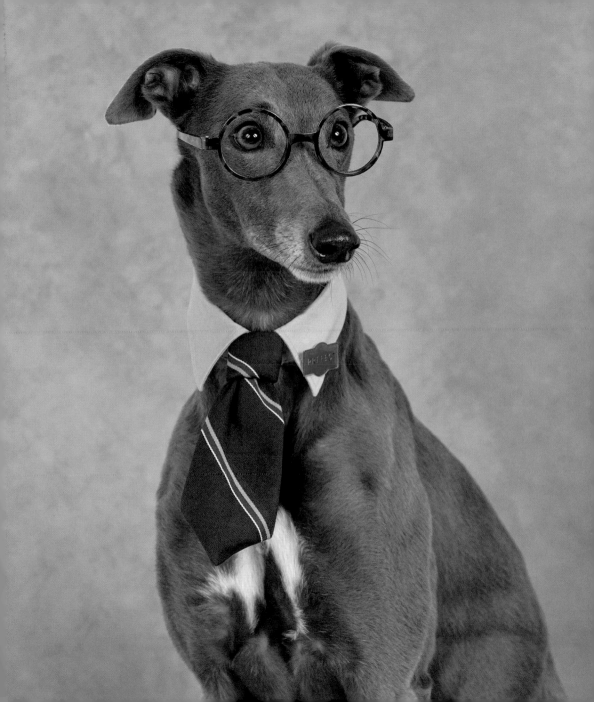

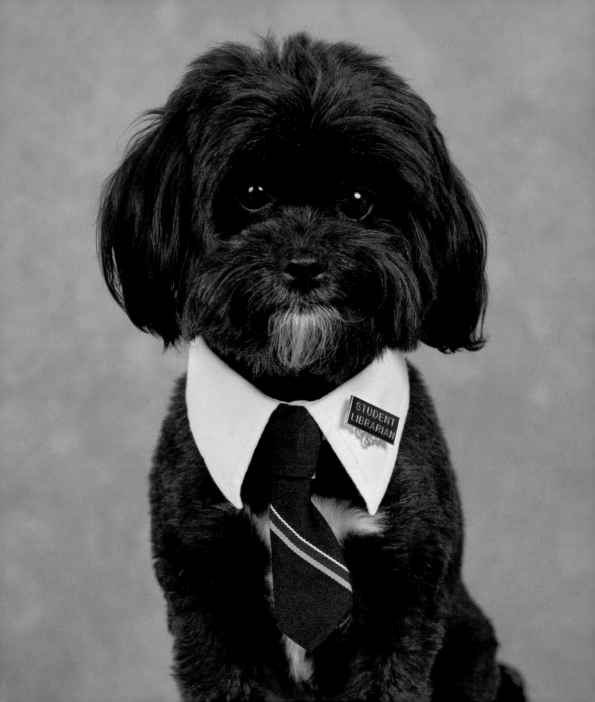

Yes, I did my homework. And, yes, I ate it.

<u>Luna</u>

My electives this year are stick-chewing and hole-digging.

Pinchy

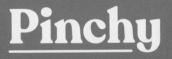

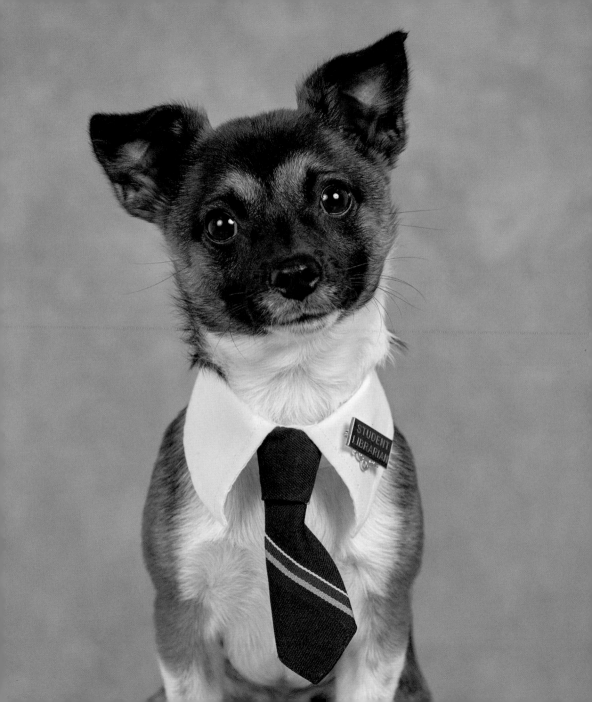

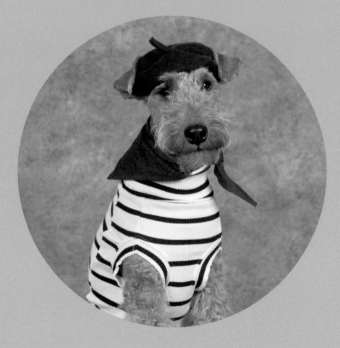

L'ARTISTE

I'm all about that joie de vivre.

<u>Bucky</u>

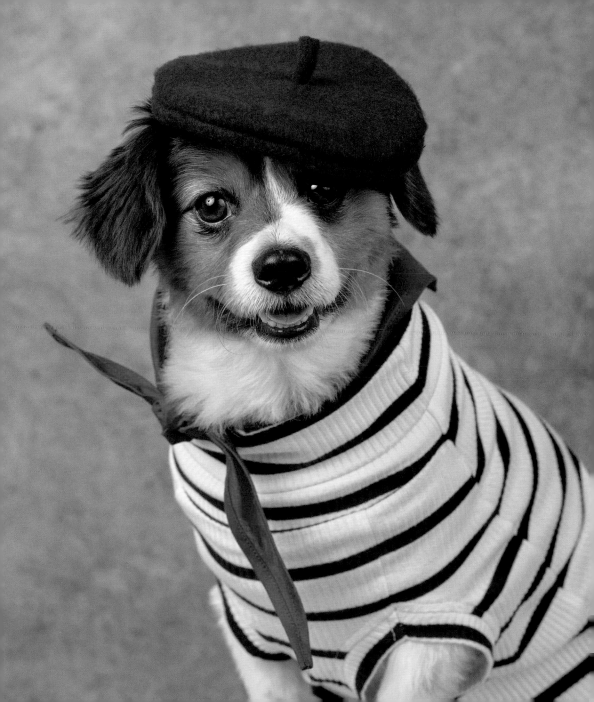

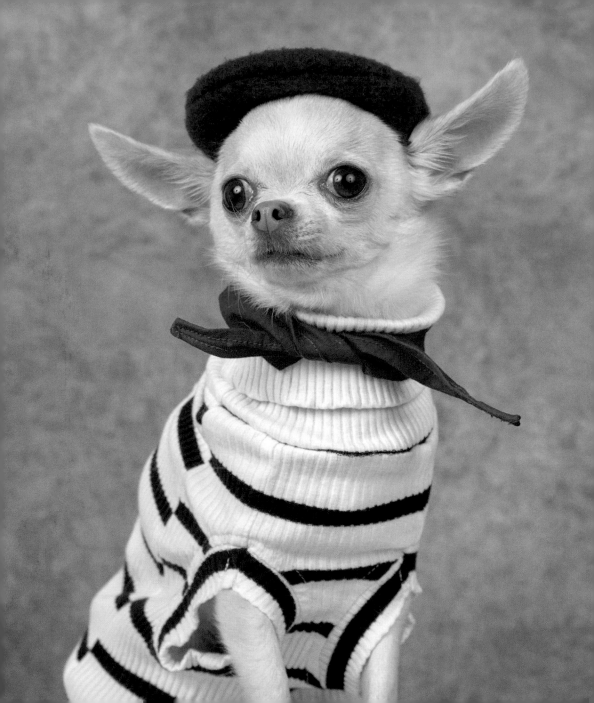

Is 'petit garçon' French for 'big ears'?

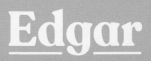

J'adore performance, visual art and experimental music.

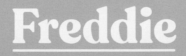

Freddie

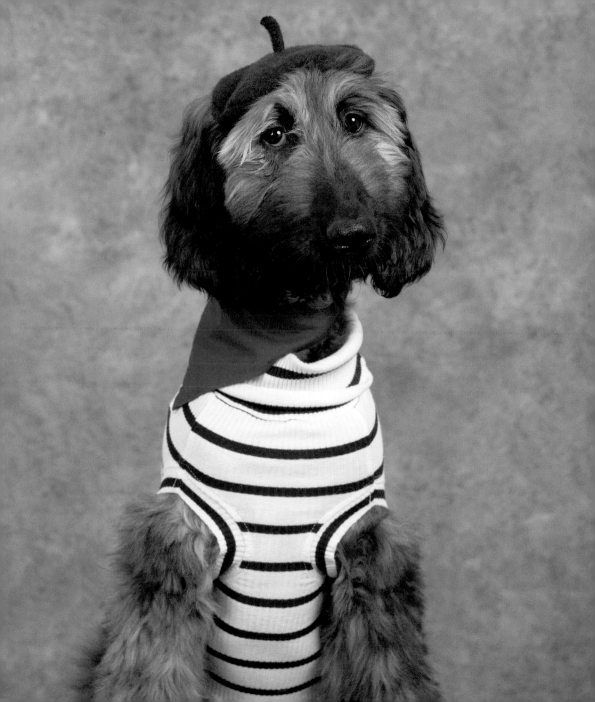

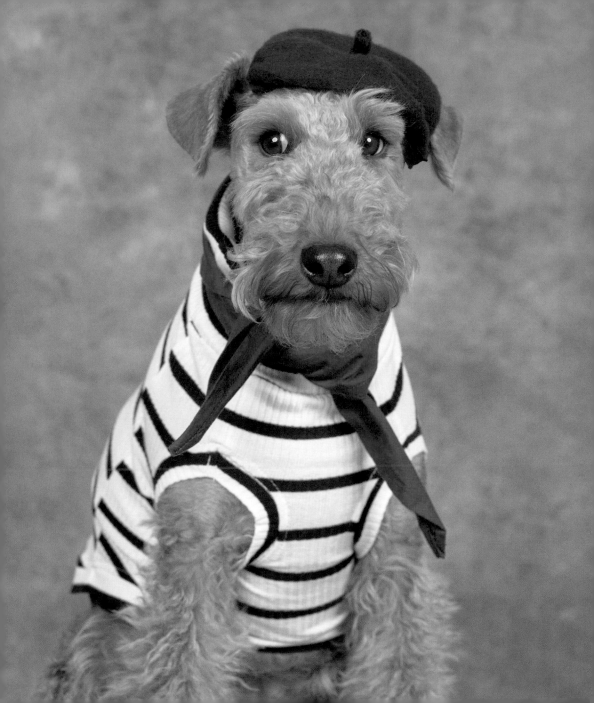

It was just a little croissant, and it was just sitting there ...

Maisy

Les enfants terribles.

Pablo and Juniper

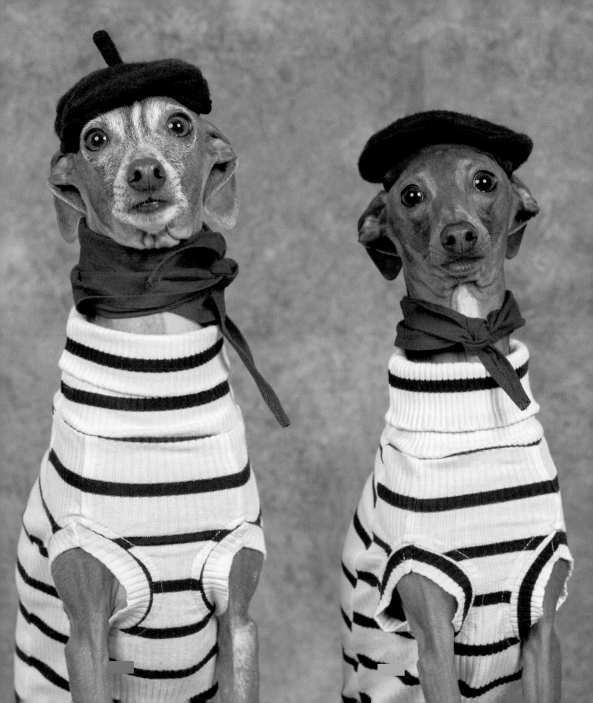

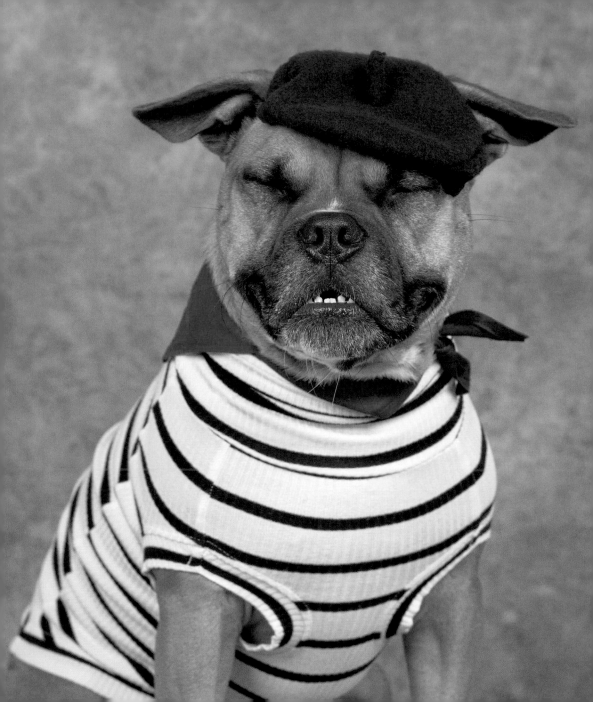

Mon Dieu!

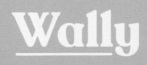

Even side-eye is better when French.

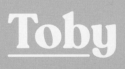

Toby

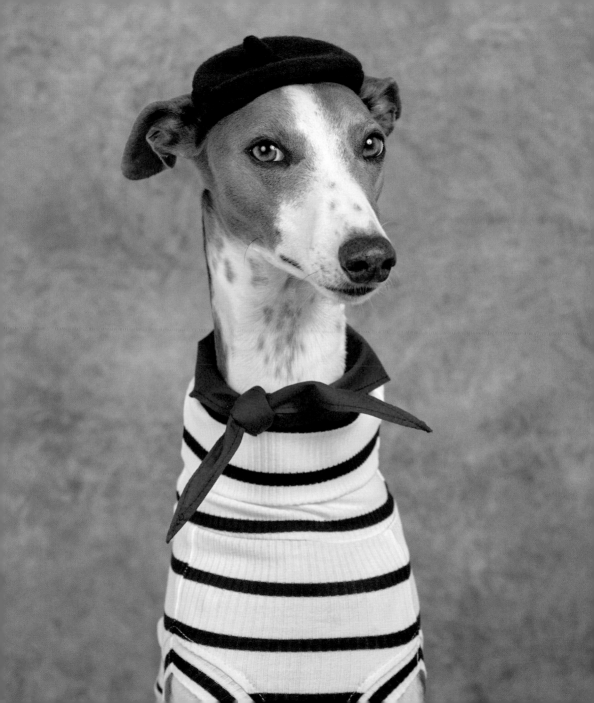

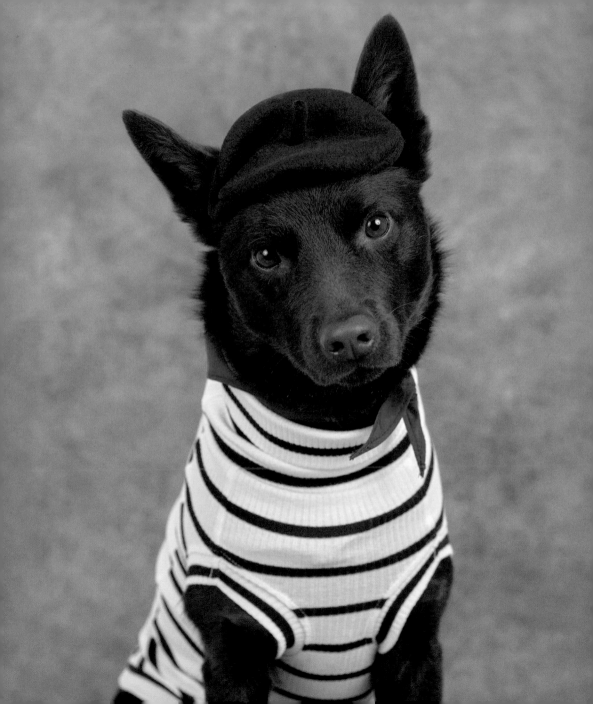

My early work explored the rare paw-print technique.

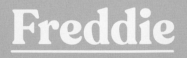

Freddie

Vive les crêpes!

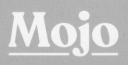

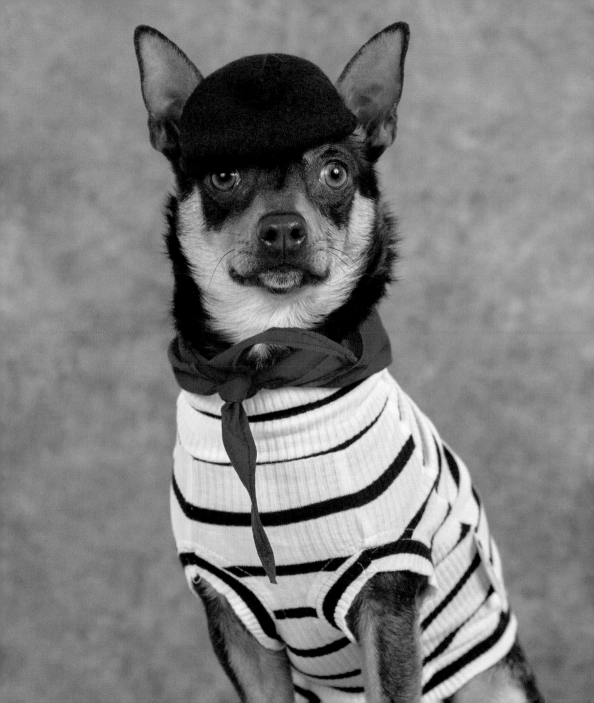

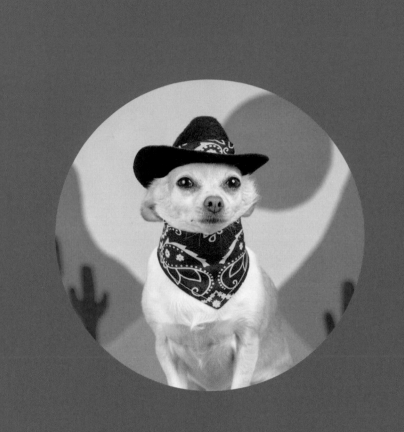

HOWDY, PARTNER!

Like a rhinestone cowgirl.

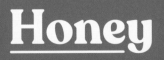

Honey

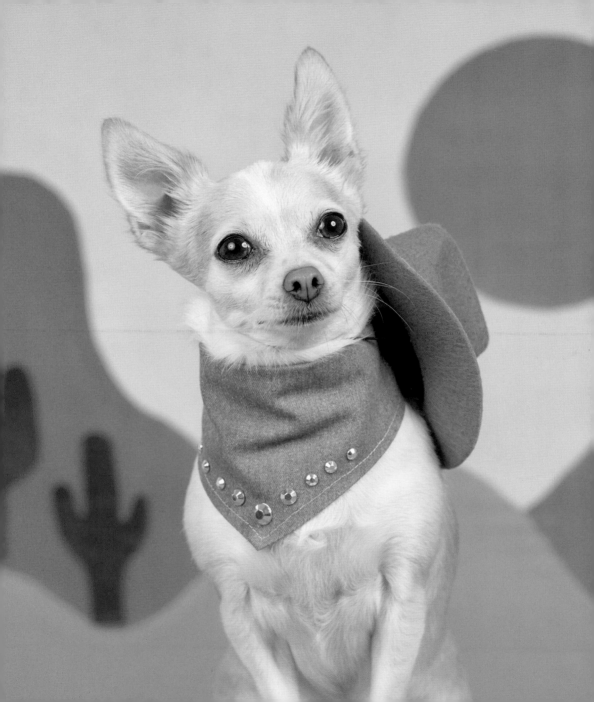

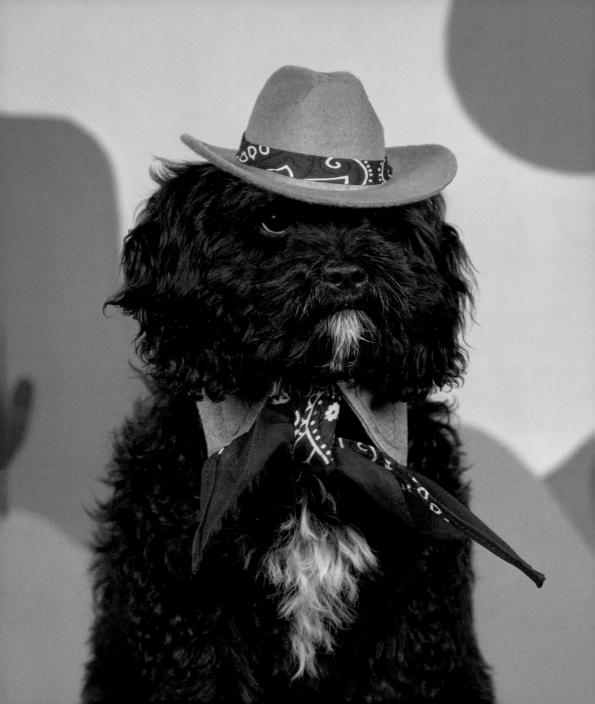

Hand over all them treatos and no one gets hurt.

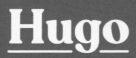

Hugo

Nobody calls *me* Mad Dog.

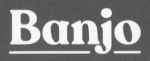

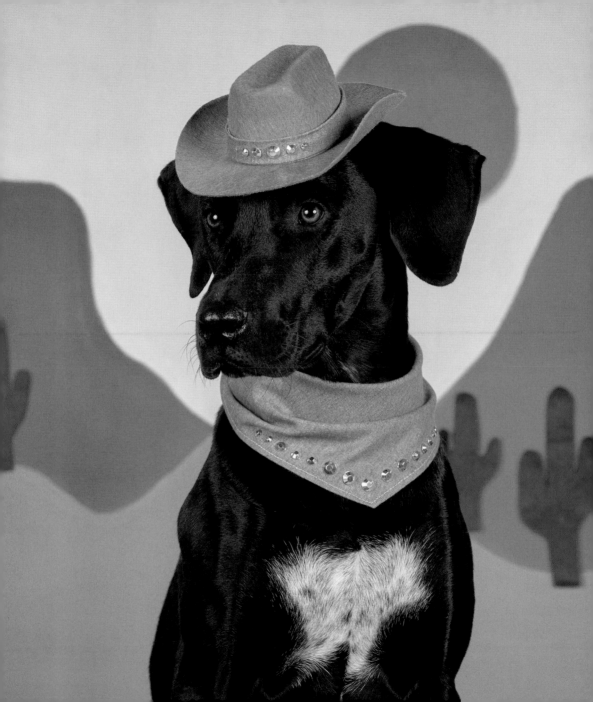

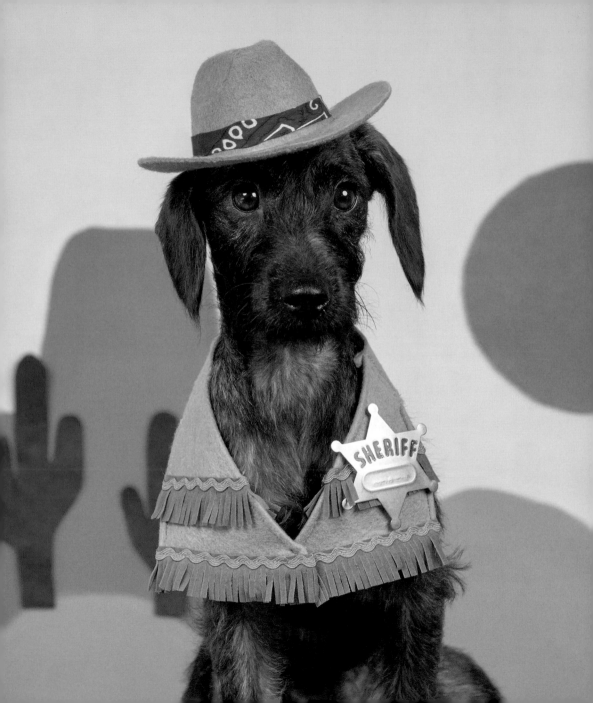

I'm not lookin' for no trouble. Just cuddles.

Scottie Puppin

Outlaws beware, there's an ankle-biter on the loose!

<u>Harry</u>

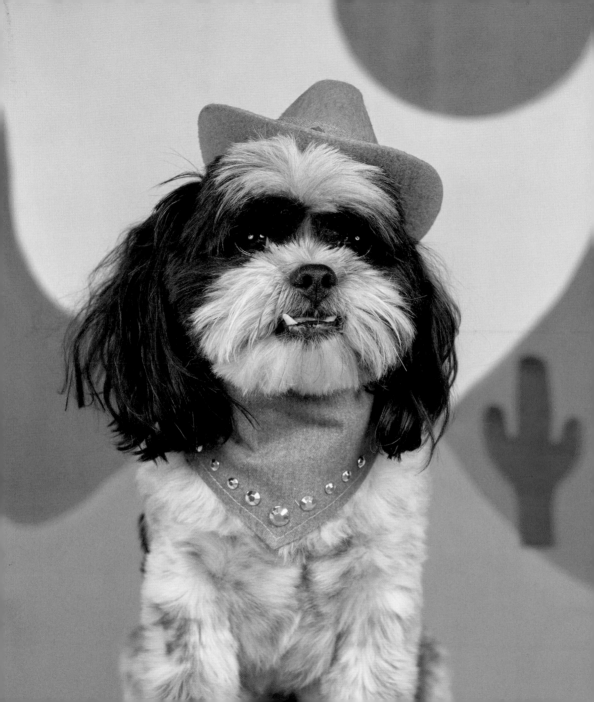

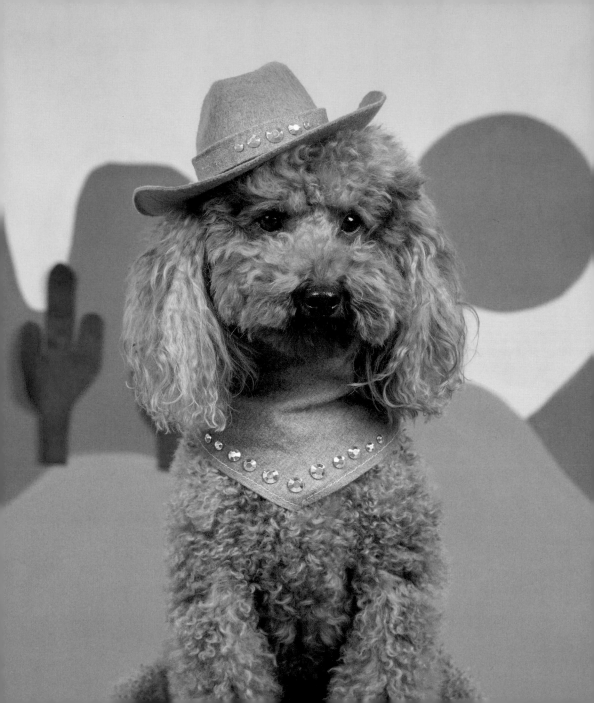

I might have added one too many studs.

Ted

Home is where I hang my hat.

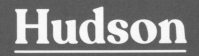

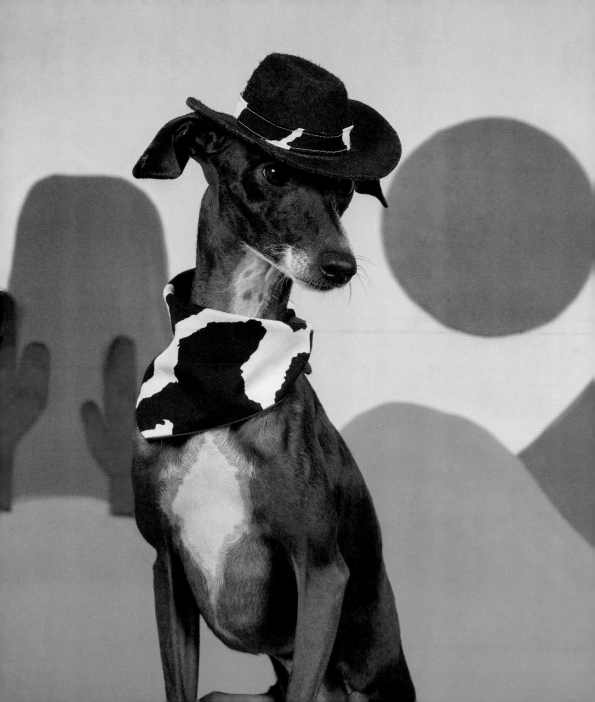

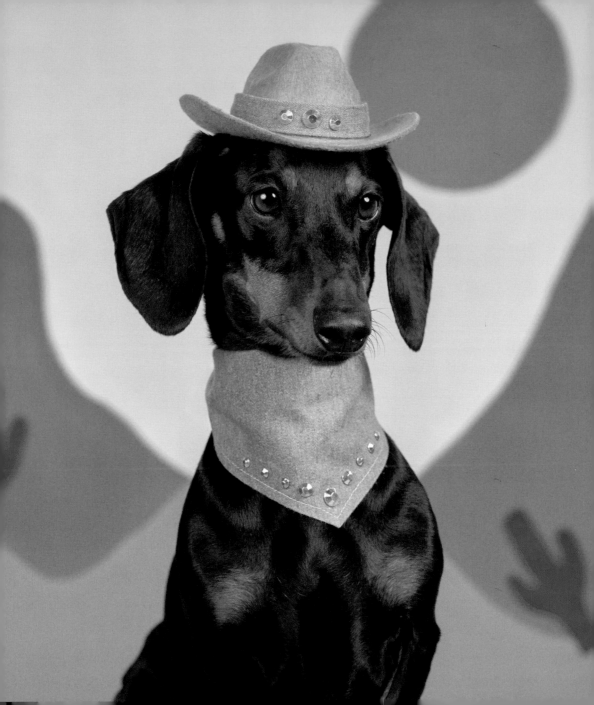

A duel at dawn? You betcha!

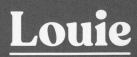

Louie

Are you even a cowboy if you don't wear a heck-load of fringing?

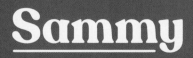

Sammy

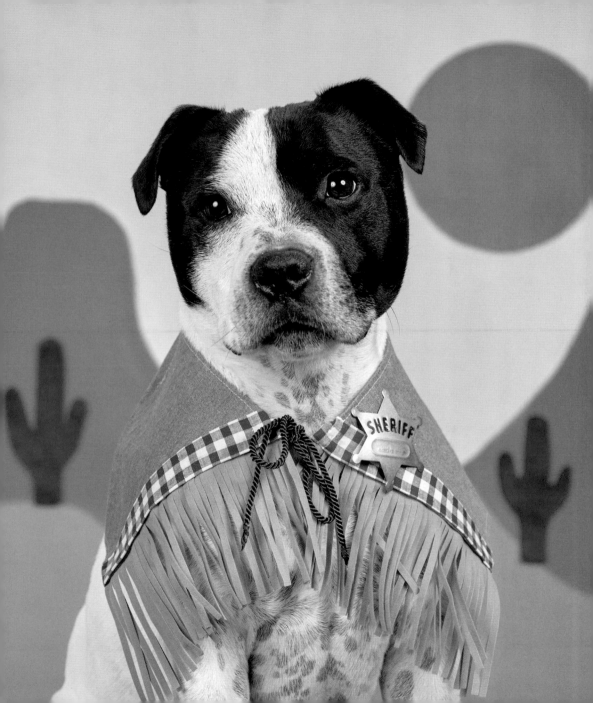

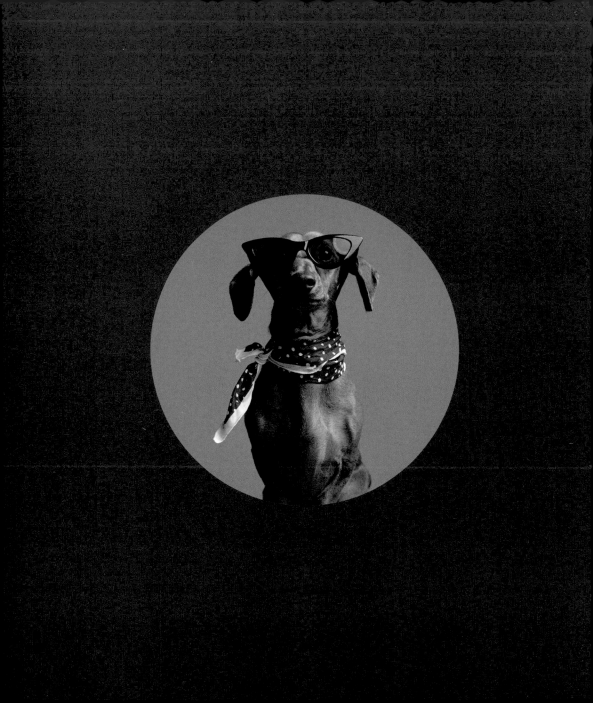

COUTURE

Why, yes, this is vintage Givenchy.

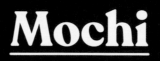

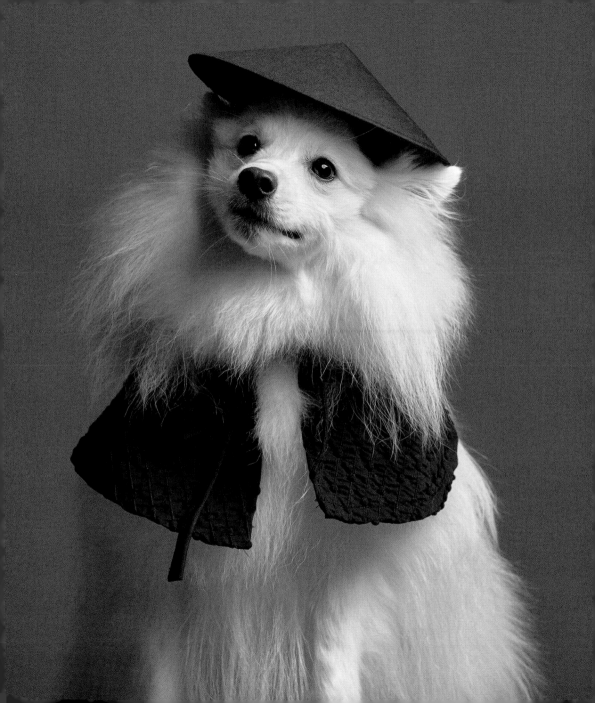

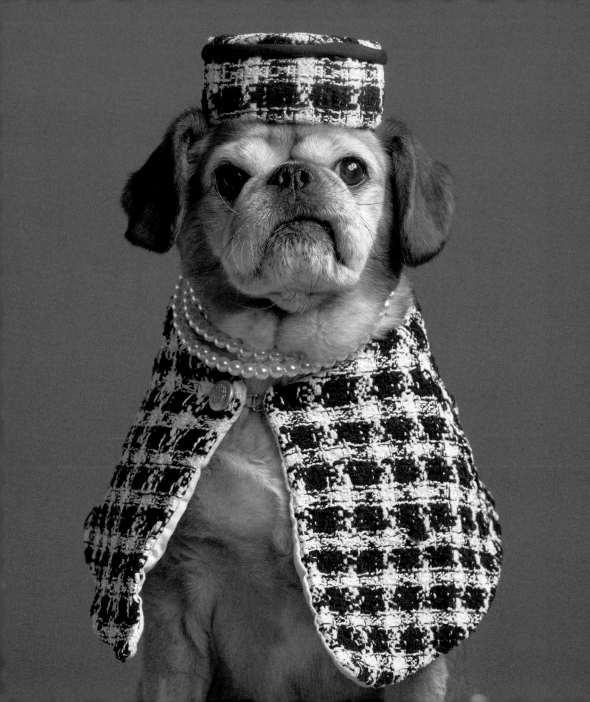

Jackie Kennedy was right: pearls are *always* appropriate.

<u>Sadie</u>

This piece is from my faux-fur collection for dogs who crave a little extra ... fur.

<u>**Baxter**</u>

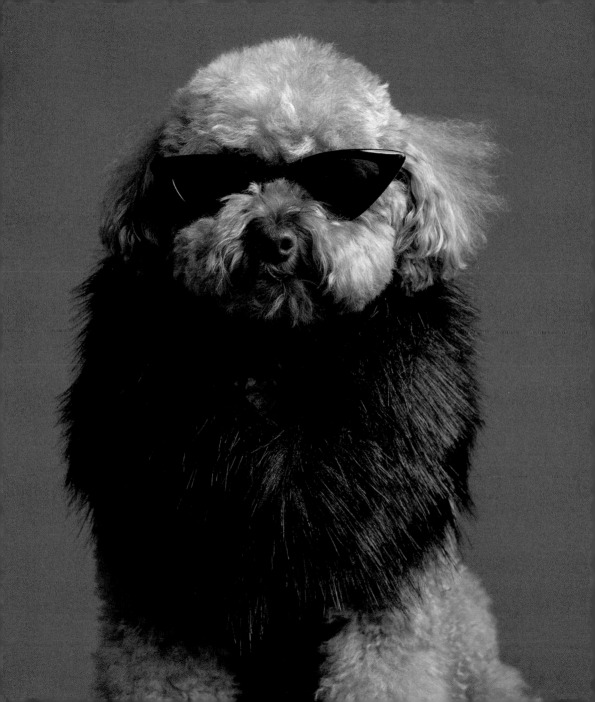

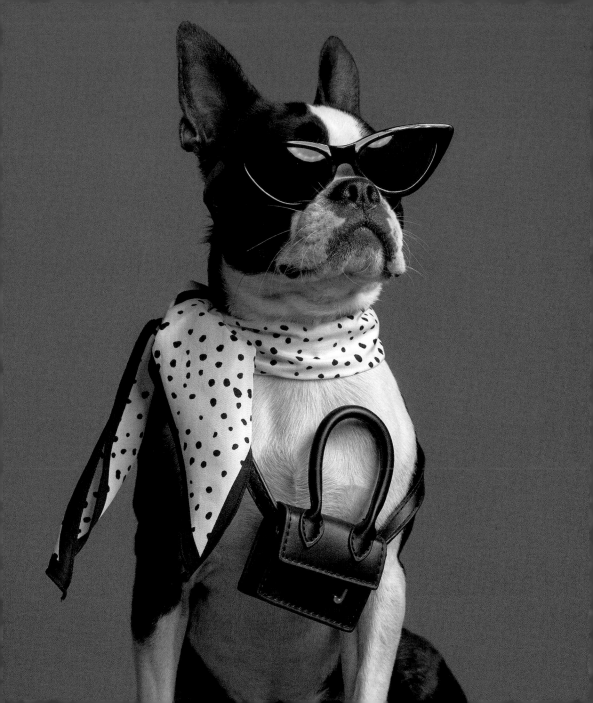

Sweetie, darling, sweetie.

<u>Lola</u>

I don't follow trends – I create them.

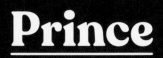

Prince

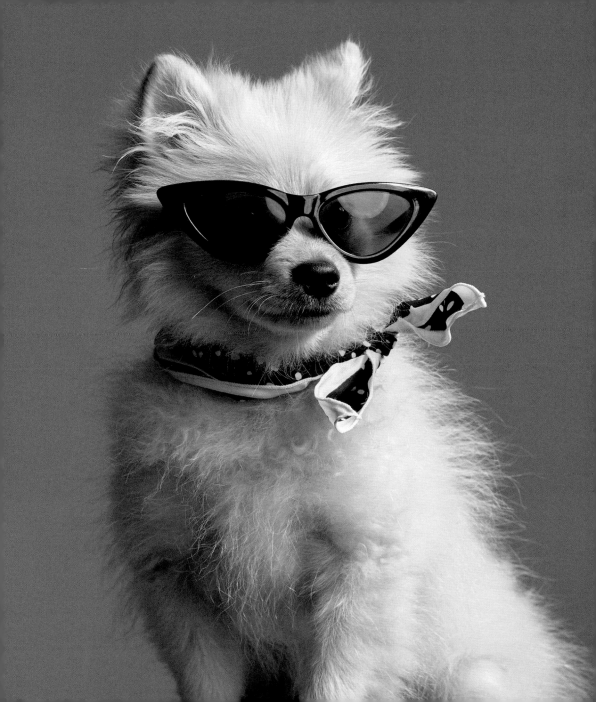

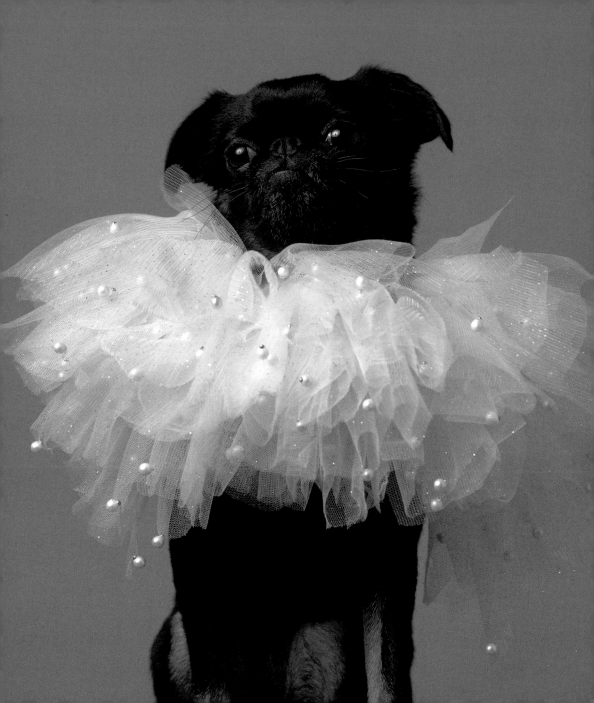

It's all about proportion. If you wear ruffles up top, wear nothing below.

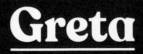

<u>Greta</u>

Coco Chanel always said that before you leave the house you should remove one thing.
I chose my pants.

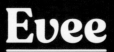

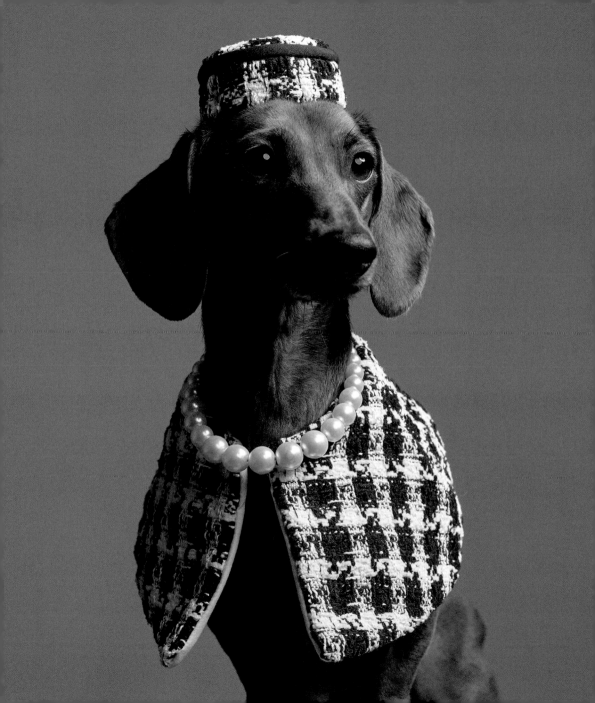

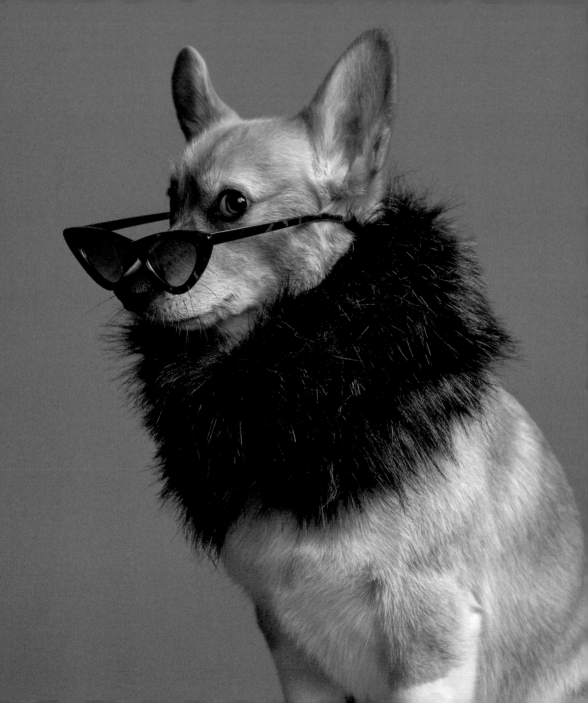

Florals for spring, you say? Groundbreaking.

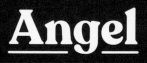

I am in mourning ... for your outfit.

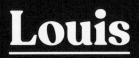

Louis

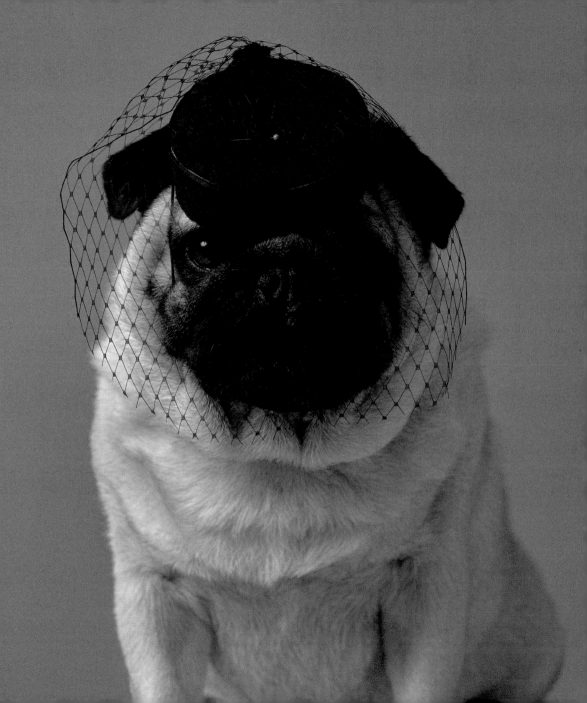

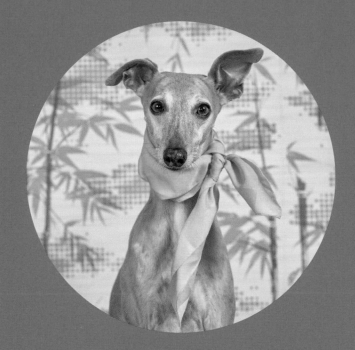

GROOVY, BABY!

Sunshine is my favourite accessory.

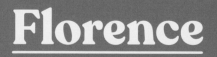

Florence

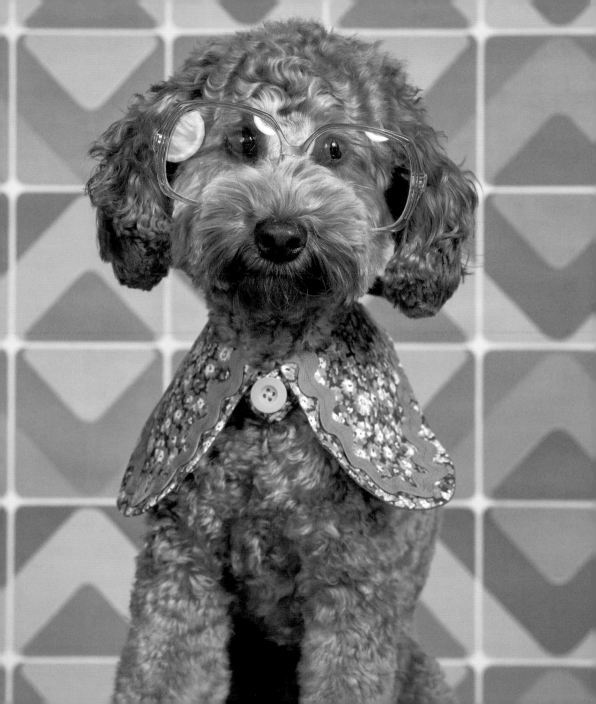

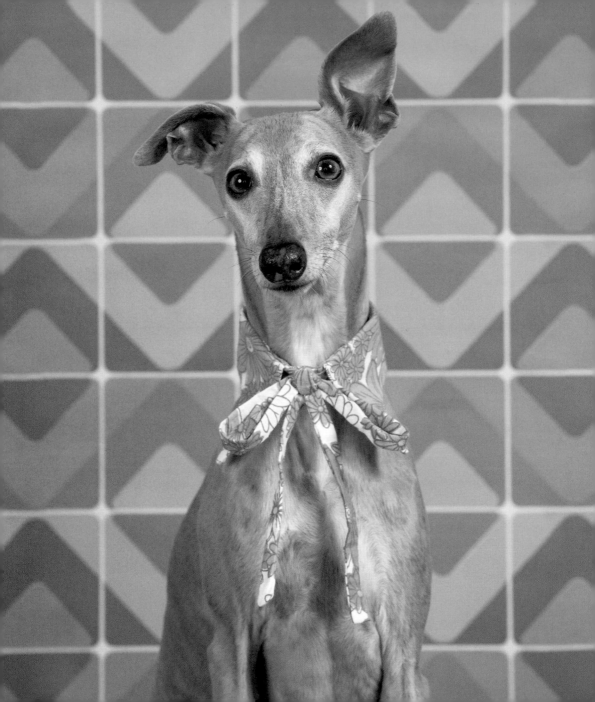

Put your ear up if you believe in peace, love and park time.

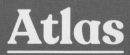

Atlas

I reject materialism ... but also really love hats and fine silks.

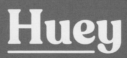

Huey

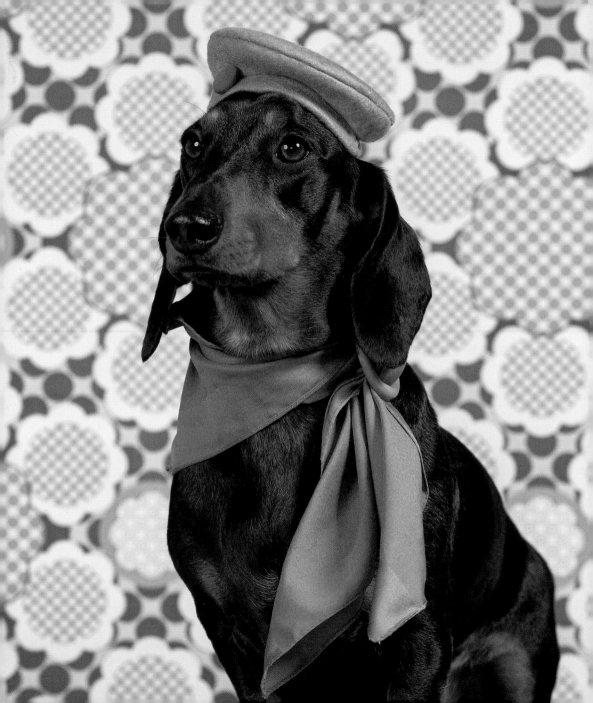

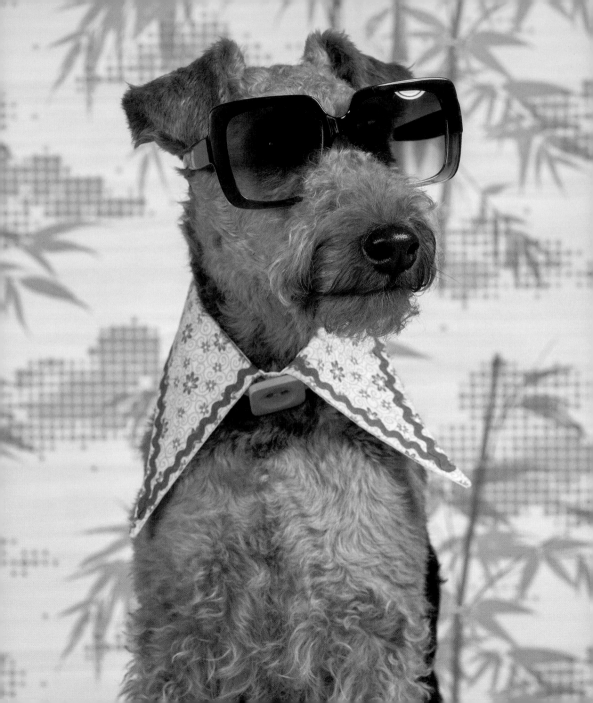

I like to view life through brown-and-green-coloured glasses.

Fozzie

Bad vibes don't go with my outfit.

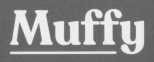

Muffy

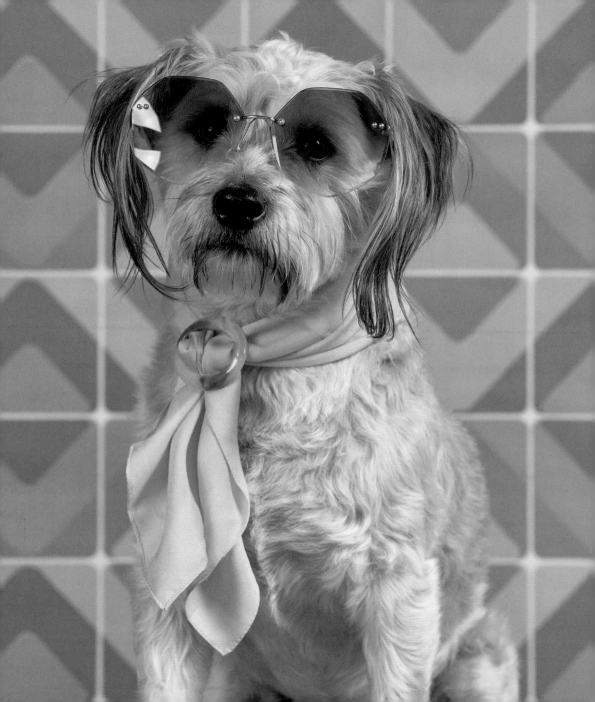

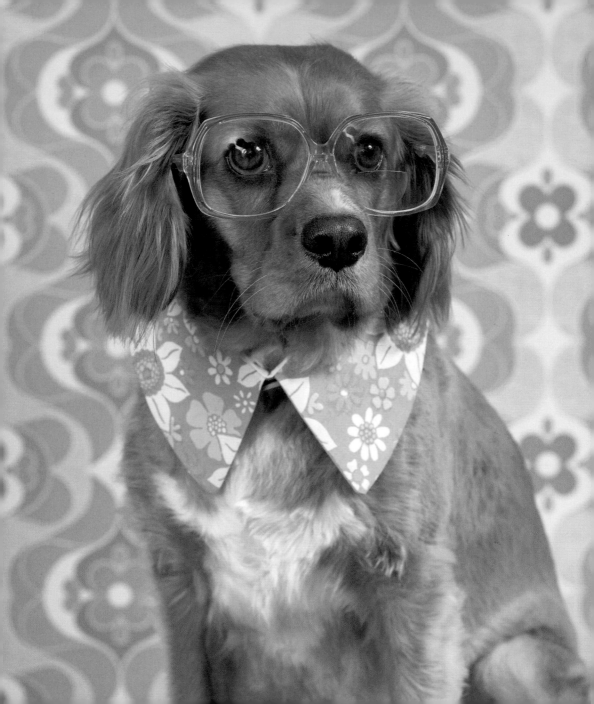

It's hard to be hip when you're the most serious dog on the scene.

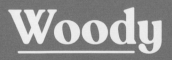

Woody

Is it still flower power if you dig up all the flowers and eat the dirt?

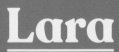

Lara

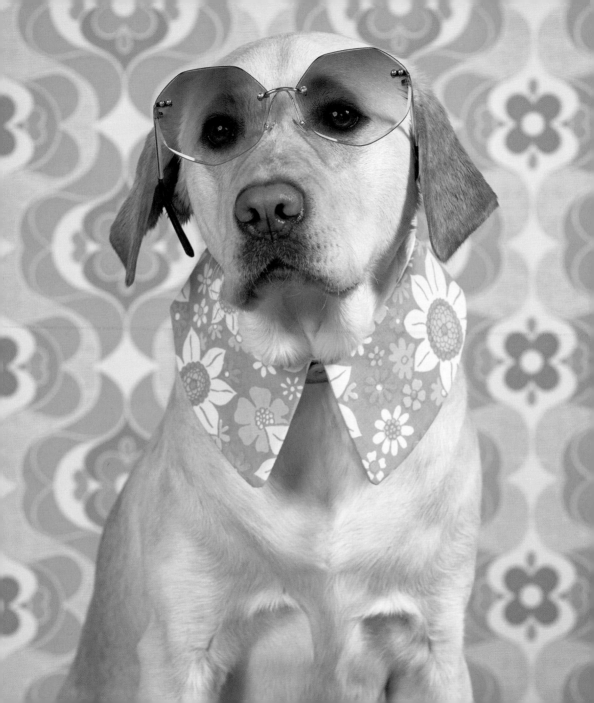

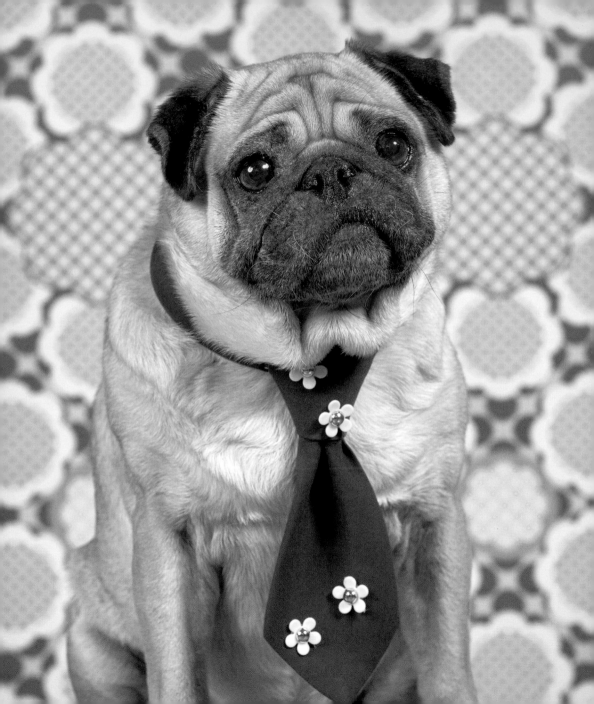

I'm worried that the flowers on my tie are too much.

Pugsley

Good vibes and tummy rubs only.

Myfanwy

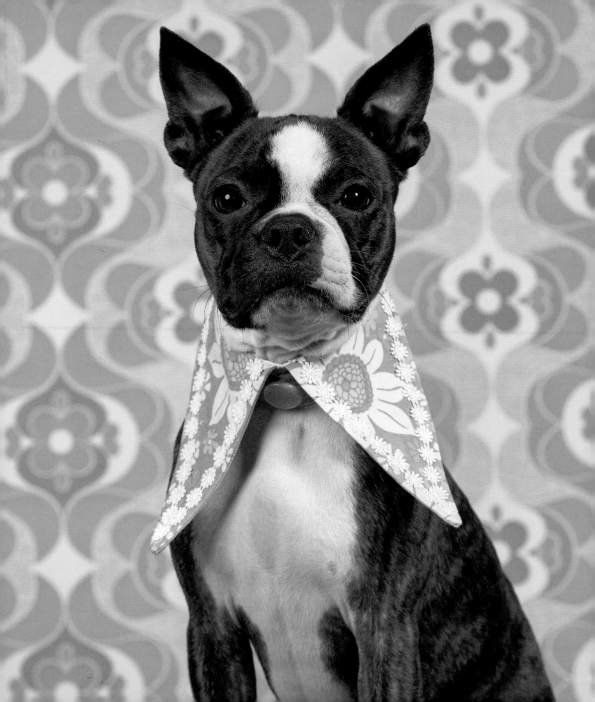

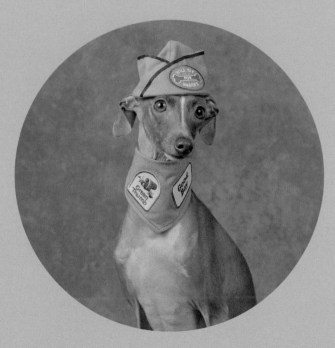

SCOUT'S
HONOUR

So, you're saying I make a fire with the stick, not *eat* the stick?

Neato

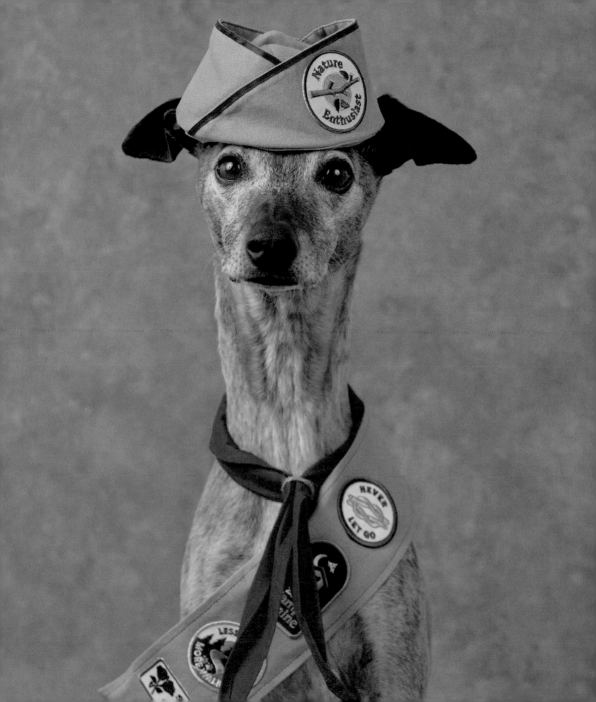

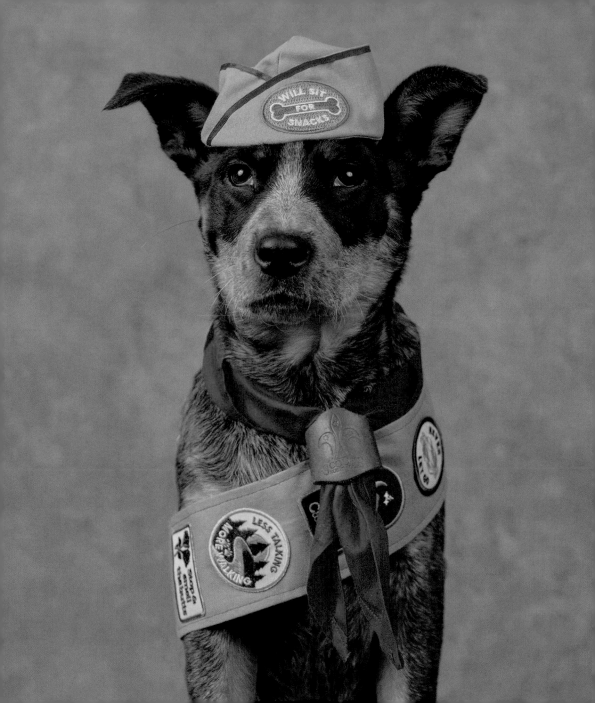

Only serious scouts need apply.

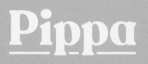

Can you be a sock thief and a good boy? I think so.

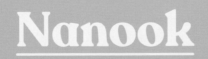

Nanook

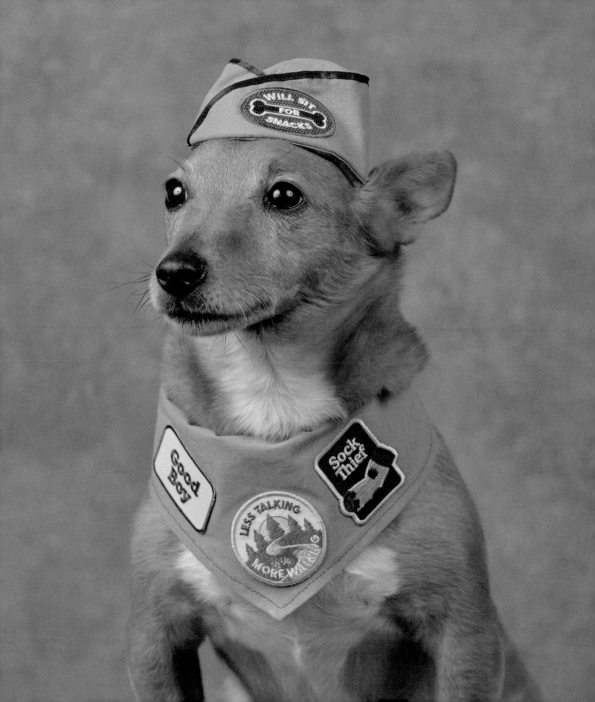

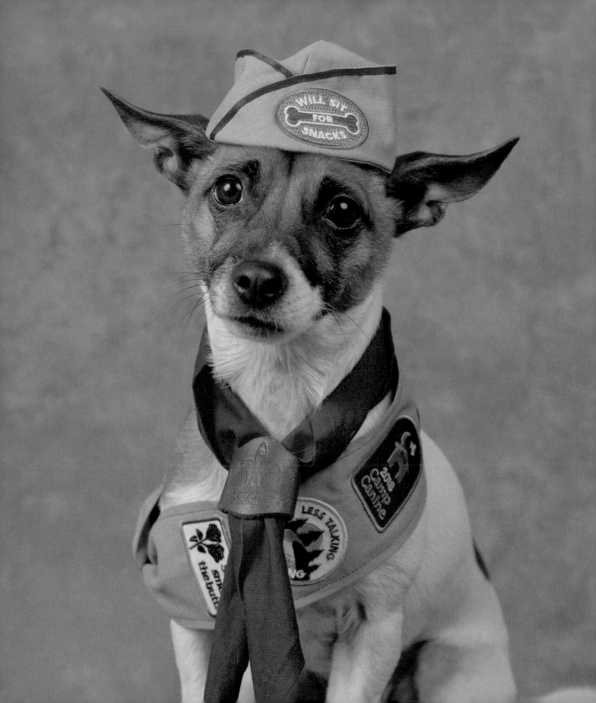

Camping? I've made a HUGE mistake.

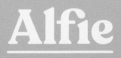

Alfie

What comes after the prestigious 'Good Boy' badge?

Chester

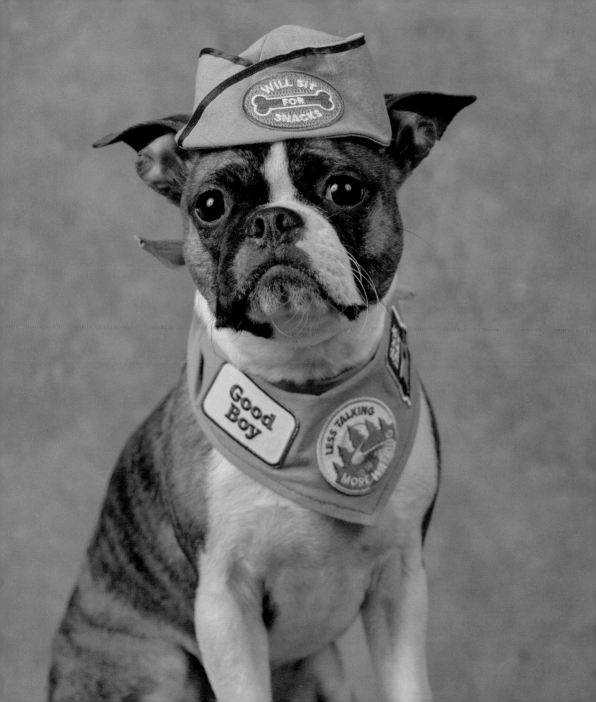

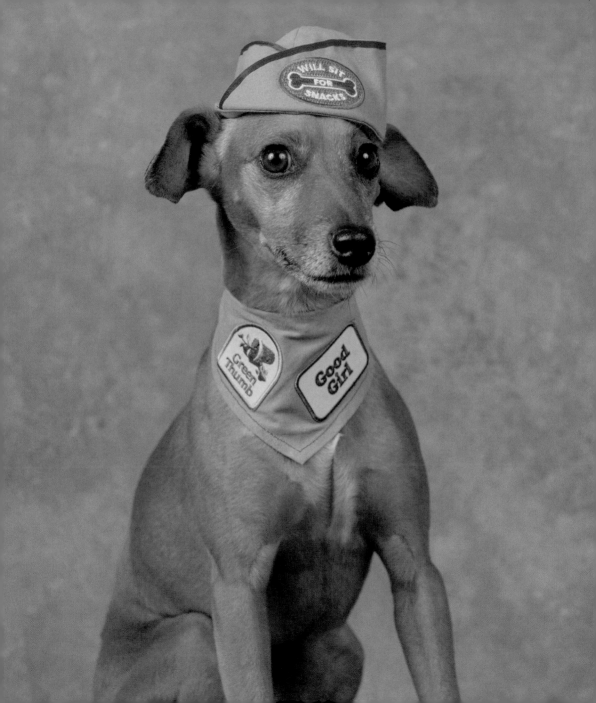

First female scout leader. Break that grass ceiling.

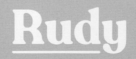
Rudy

I didn't chop this wood, but I did pee on it.

<u>Pablo</u>

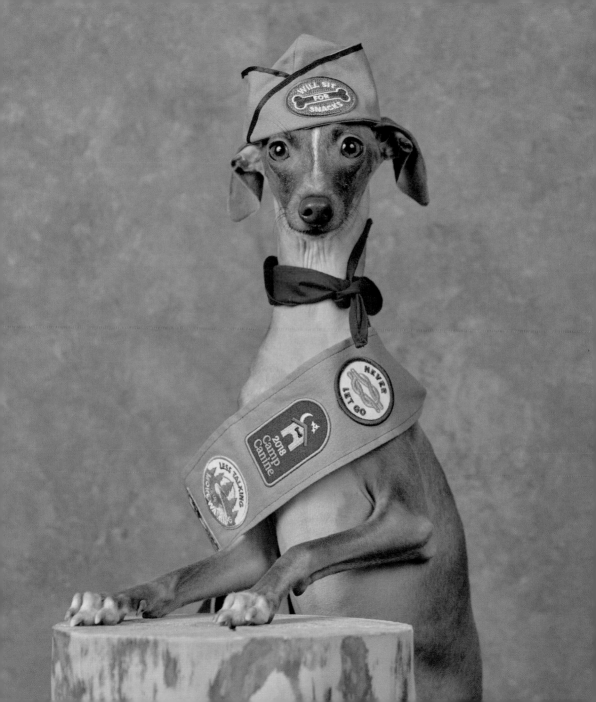

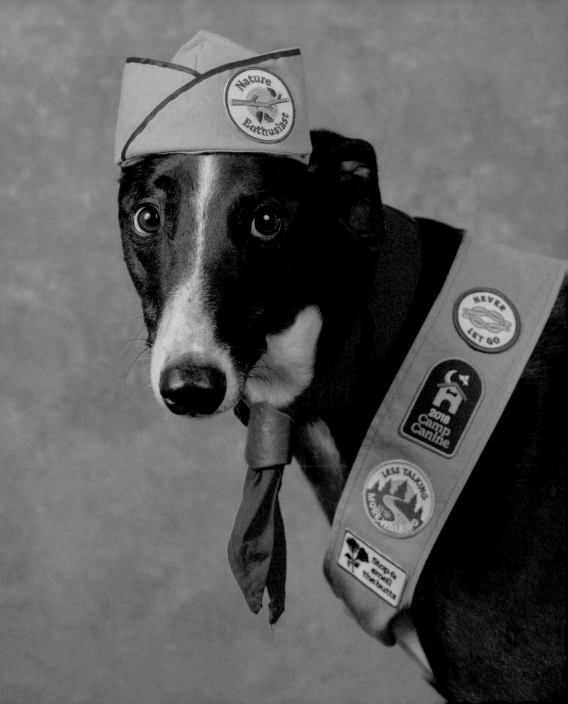

I still don't understand why the tents don't have orthopedic beds.

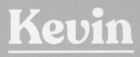

Kevin

Do these hats come in a smaller size?

Delilah

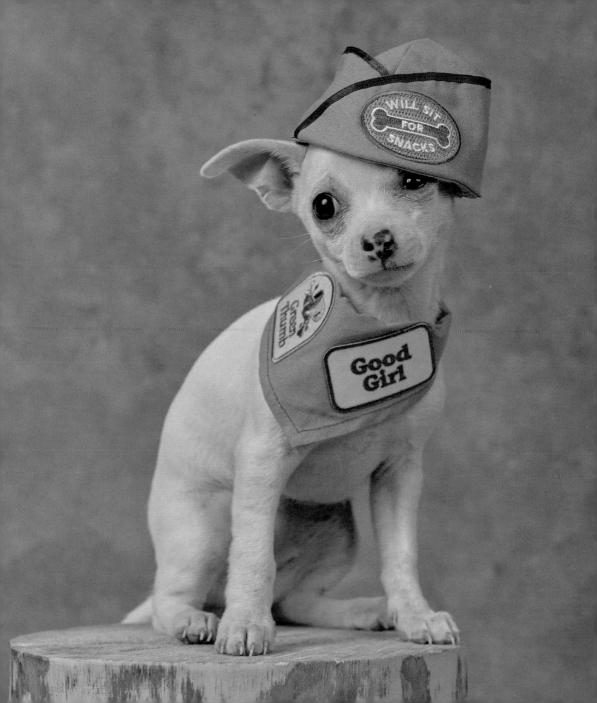

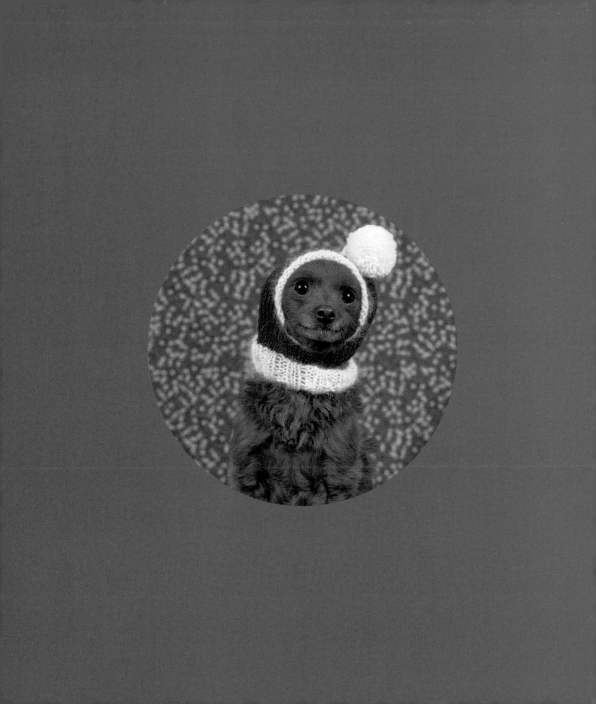

NAUGHTY OR NICE?

Up early with Christmas-morning hair to get my presents.

Mr Bingley

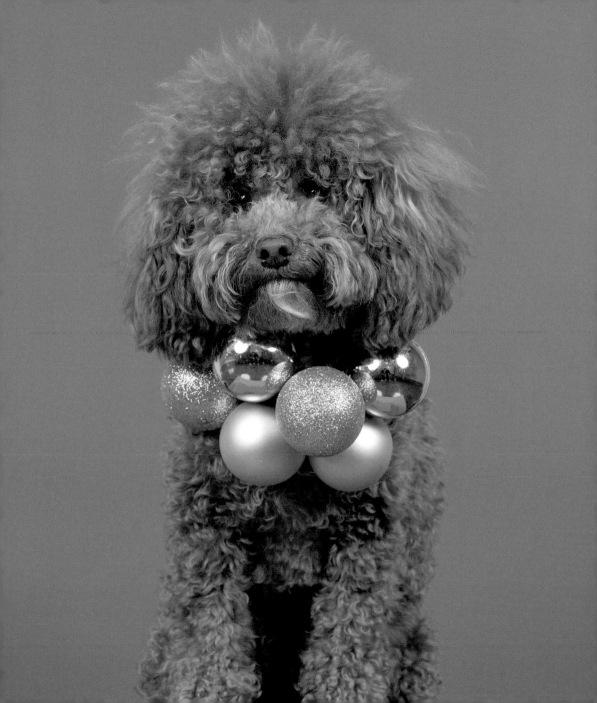

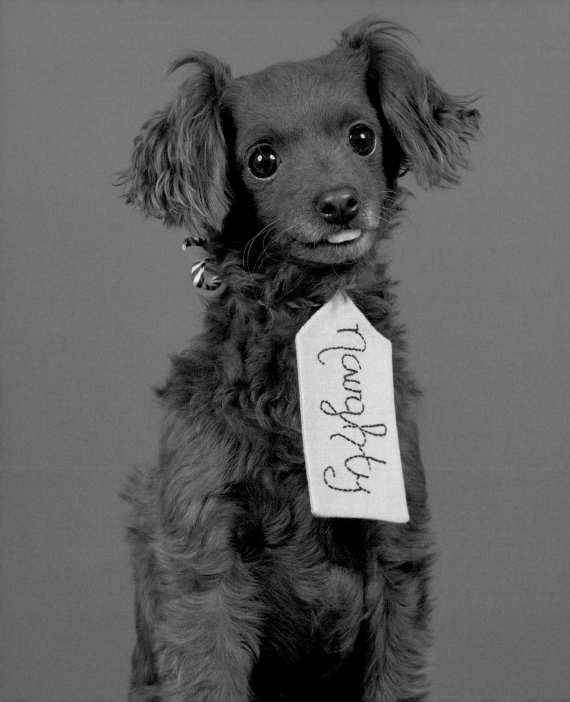

Naughty or nice? Like it matters when you are this cute.

Bill

Merry Christmas. I ate the turkey.

Maggie

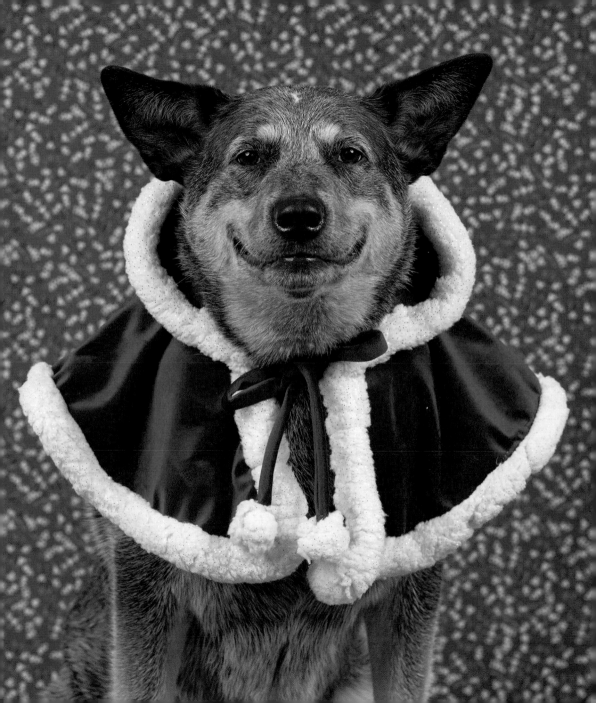

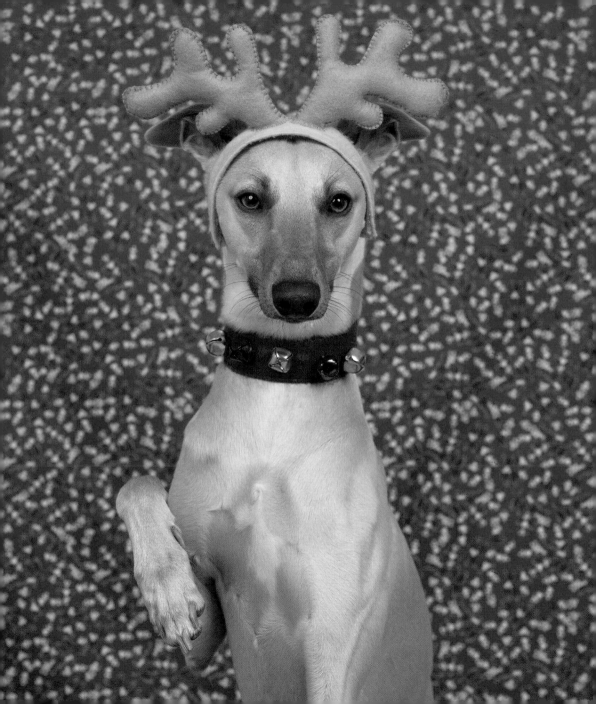

What's even cuter than reindeer? Rein-dogs!

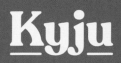

Channelling all my Christmas-tree energy.

Yeji

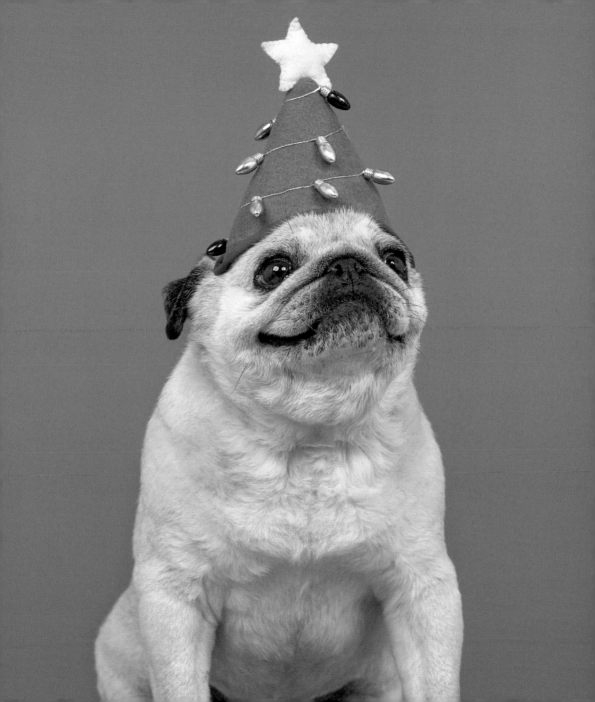

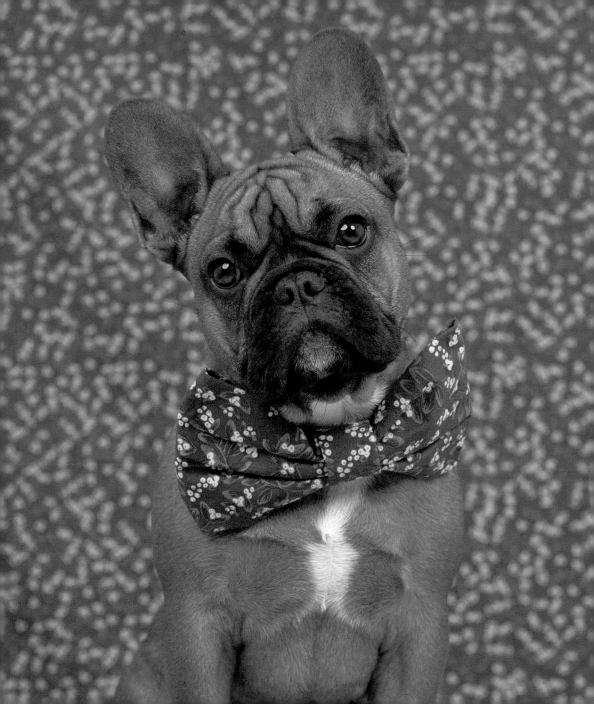

I was so worried about missing out on Christmas dinner that I gave myself three new wrinkles.

Slim

Who're you calling Pudding?

Aggie

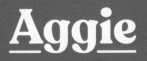

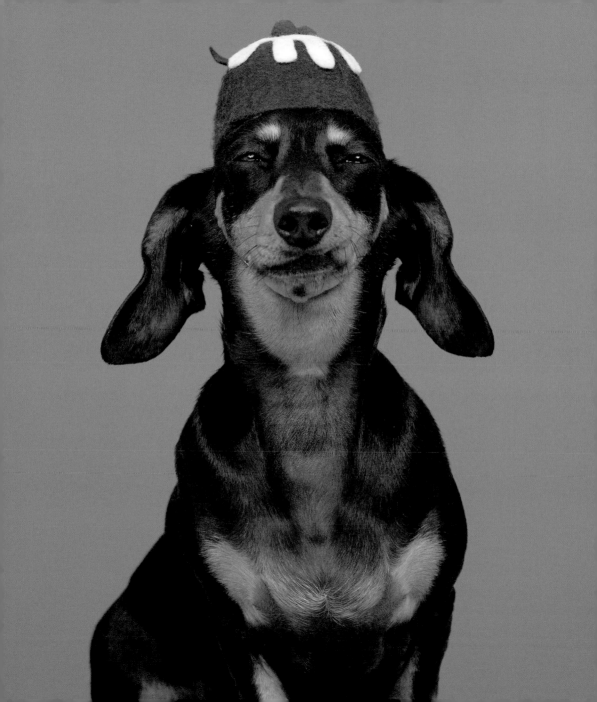

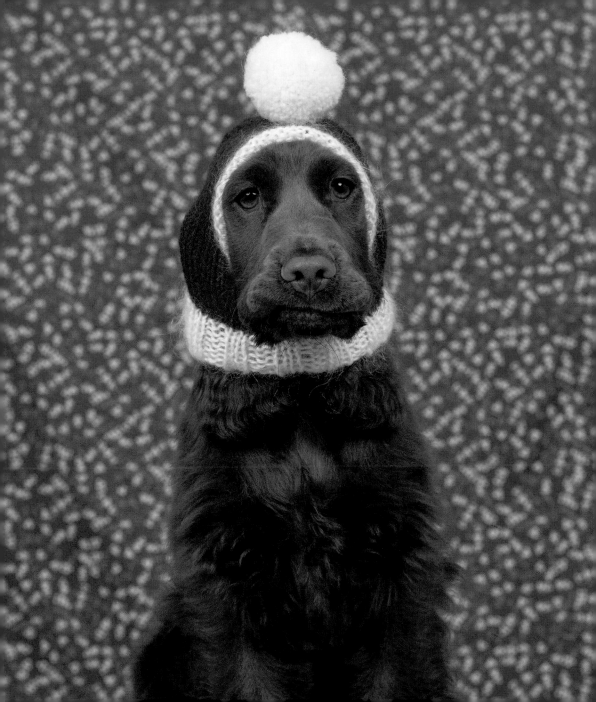

This year, Santa, I'd like new parents, please.

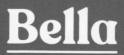

Bella

Why, yes, I DO love presents!

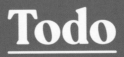

Todo

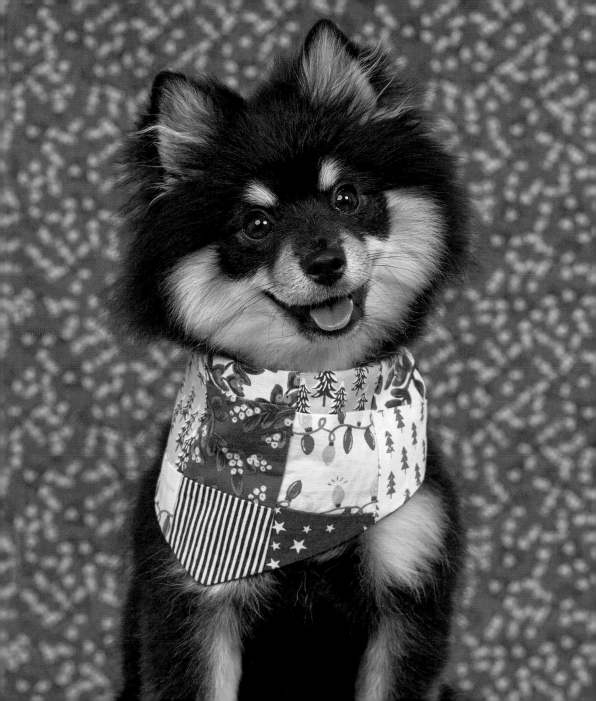

Harper *by* Design

An imprint of HarperCollins*Publishers*

Australia • Brazil • Canada • France • Germany
Holland • India • Italy • Japan • Mexico • New Zealand
Poland • Spain • Sweden • Switzerland
United Kingdom • United States of America

HarperCollins acknowledges the Traditional
Custodians of the land upon which we live and
work, and pays respect to Elders past and present.

First published on Gadigal Country in Australia
in 2023 by HarperCollins*Publishers* Australia
Pty Limited
ABN 36 009 913 517
harpercollins.com.au

A catalogue record for this book is available from
the National Library of Australia

ISBN 978 1 4607 6599 9

Publisher: Mark Campbell
Publishing Director: Brigitta Doyle
Designer: Mietta Yans, HarperCollins Design Studio
Front and back cover images: Dog Photog
Colour reproduction by Splitting Image Colour
Studio, Wantirna, Victoria
Printed and bound in China by 1010 Printing on
128gsm matt art

8 7 6 5 4 3 2   24 25 26 27

Banjo's caption on page 50, 'Nobody calls *me* Mad
Dog', was inspired by Buford Tannen's character
in *Back to the Future III* (screenplay by Robert
Zemeckis and Bob Gale). Angel's caption on
page 81, 'Florals for spring, you say? Groundbreaking',
was inspired by Miranda Priestly's character in
The Devil Wears Prada (novel by Lauren Weisberger,
screenplay by Aline Brosh McKenna).